HOW TO CATCH

A FALLING

KNIFE

HOW TO CATCH

A FALLING

KNIFE

Daniel Johnson

ALICE JAMES BOOKS
FARMINGTON, MAINE

10 9 8 7 6 5 4 3 2 1

Alice James Books are published by Alice James Poetry Cooperative, Inc., an affiliate
of the University of Maine at Farmington.

ALICE JAMES BOOKS
238 MAIN STREET
FARMINGTON, ME 04938

www.alicejamesbooks.org

Library of Congress Cataloging-in-Publication Data

Johnson, Daniel, 1973-
 How to catch a falling knife / Daniel Johnson.
    p. cm.
  ISBN 978-1-882295-79-1
  I. Title.
  PS3610.O333H69 2010
  811'.6--dc22
                        2010000104

Alice James Books gratefully acknowledges support from individual donors, private
foundations, the University of Maine at Farmington and the National Endowment
for the Arts. ❧

Contributions for the production of *How to Catch a Falling Knife* made by:
Michael S. Glaser

Cover art: Swetlana Heger, *Smoke (Abstraction), 2,* 2008
Color print su chrome de luxe paper, mounted on aluminum and acrylic glass,
hanging construction on the back
35 x 45 cm (13.8 x 17.7 inches)
ed 1/3
courtesy Swetlana Heger and EFFEARTE Gallery

CONTENTS

ACKNOWLEDGMENTS

88: A Journal of Contemporary American Poetry: "First"

American Letters & Commentary: "0"

Barrow Street: "Do Unto Others" and "Father Song"

Boston Review: "Description of a Badly Drawn Horse"

Best American Poetry 2007: "Do Unto Others" (reprinted with
    permission)

Forklift, Ohio: "After Life"

Hinchas de Poesía: "Lightweight Champion of the World"

Iowa Review: "For Ebele"

Notre Dame Review: "Insomniac's Psalm" and "Miniature"

Pierogi Press: "After Words" and "Errata"

Poetry Daily: "Description of a Badly Drawn Horse" (reprinted with
    permission)

Spoon River Poetry Review: "Her Body Is a White Thing in the Sun Now"

VERSE: "Visitation" and "The Reflection of All Visible Light"

For cutting a poet a paycheck, I am grateful to 826 Boston, Snow City
Arts Foundation, and Young Chicago Authors. For offering a desk, a
bed, and so much more, my gratitude to the Vermont Studio Center
and to the Warren Wilson College MFA Program for Writers. I thank
the following people for their unflagging friendship and support: Rachel
Webster, Scott Challener, Colleen Abel, Gary Lilley, Josie Raney, James
Foley, Yago Said-Cura, Jenn Morea, Paul Sznewajs, Sadia Uqaili, the
Okpokwasili family, Tom Durkin, Edwin Gonzalez, and Jim Savage.

My teachers– Jeanne E. Clark, Chris Forhan, Matthea Harvey, Li Young Lee, and Heather McHugh—I salute you! To Carey, Bill, and the Alice James crew, thank you for shepherding my work into print. Ebele, *ezigbo nwunyem*—sorry I wrecked your car in Maine.

For my family

What's left after what one isn't is taken away is what one is.

–Diane Arbus,
1959 Notebook (Vol. I)

I am easy to define.
Seeing devoured me.

–Fernando Pessoa

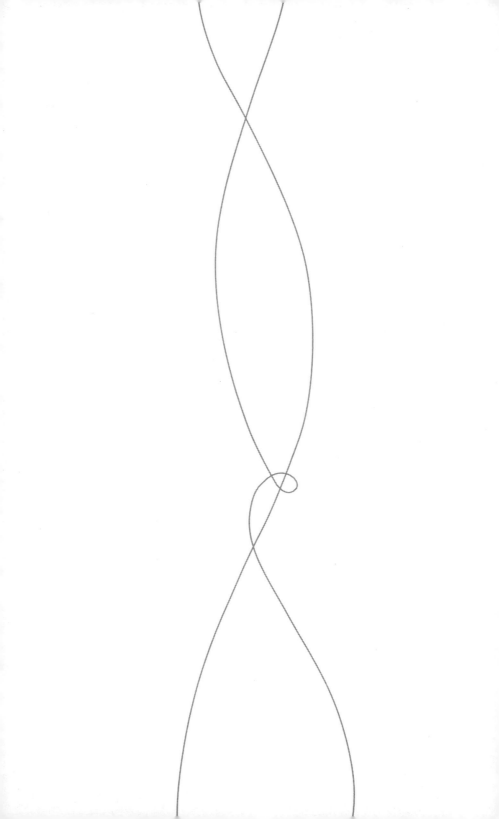

ACCOUNTING FOR THE WREN, THE ROCKET, AND THE IMMATERIAL

The sky becomes what is added to it—
       a radio tower, stratus clouds, one hundred Chinese kites,

until one day, a day like today when winds gust east, then
       west, blowing hard off the lake,

the sky becomes what is taken away—

       a vapor trail vanished: the absence of geese: a gaping
       space where before there was none.

Begin again the slow math of loss. Use feathers, flint,
       a scattering of seeds,

until the sky, once more, fills with that which is offered to it—

       our love-cries and curses, our Kaddishes, our longing
and singing, our long, long keening.

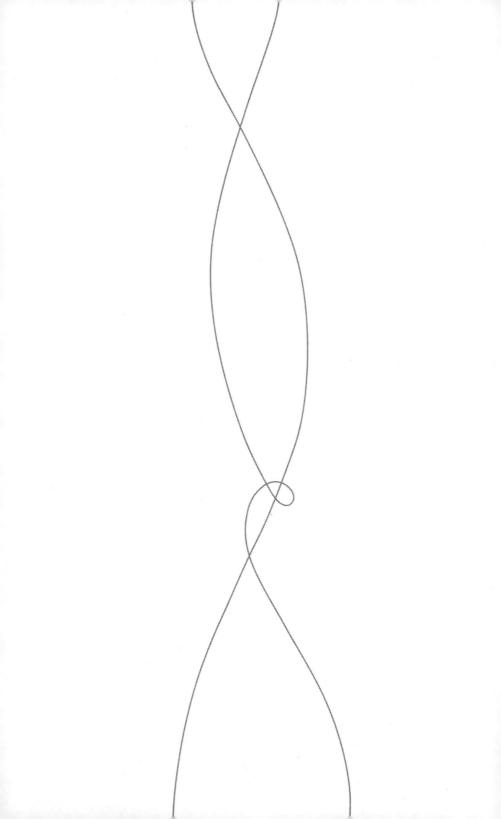

FIRST

What struck me first was their panic—
how tangled in hoses my father,
swabbing muck from my eyes,
clutched me like a baby
gorilla: unsure whether
to hold me or hurl me.
Under the angels' white lights,
my mother shrieked; my sister
leaked tears for fourteen floors.
Black day, black day, was all
my brother could mutter.

Then, quick and blue, I saw
my first bird: again and again,
beating its beauty against
the clear windows of my new home.

VISITATION

Smoke smeared the sky.
The sun was a hole,

but my mother wouldn't believe
the river was burning.

Another drowned twin,
a two-headed perch perhaps,

but water, brown and crooked
as it was, still wouldn't catch.

Must be a mill fire, she countered.
Streetlights blinking on. The bridge

backed up with rusty cars.
From Strongsville to Cuyahoga,

a steelworker crawled on his knees.
At supper, nothing was said.

The Crooked River on fire–
Christ would return on a barge.

NORTH LIFE

−40° 53' 48" E, 80° 49' 52" N

One came as sunlight slanting through pine smoke.
Another took the face of an hour's rain; a third
emerged as a flock of birds circling the dump.
Little, we suspected little, picking apples
already part wine. We smoked cloves, hung our feet
off a railroad trestle. No thunder clapped.
No music announced coming or leaving.
Skittish and wide-eyed, they moved among us—
small town gods less terrible than our dads.
As for us, boys out of earshot, or so we thought,
we broke green bottles on rocks, M-80d a frog,
sprayed sumac with BBs, shouting into the gulch.

LIGHTWEIGHT CHAMPION OF THE WORLD

Same year I asked for boxing gloves,
Boom Boom Mancini killed a man,
a Korean boxer in yellow trunks
who went down twice in the twelfth
and didn't get up. I got the gloves anyway,
ruddy leather mitts weighing a pound a piece.
I could barely keep my dukes aloft
circling Georgie in the basement, an egg timer
ticking away on the ping-pong table.
We'd duck, bob, and duck to boos
from the stands and flying beer cups.
Our jabs died short. Lazy hooks sailed wide.
Only once did I stand over Georgie
the way I'd imagined. Blood wormed out
of his nose. His eyes fluttered shut.
I raised my gloves above my head
then ran from the house.

MY FATHER, THE SMALL TOWN SADIST

is whistling his way to the dump.
A tin pail of teeth hangs
from the handlebars of his bike,

molars and canines clacking
like shells as he steers over cobblestone.
Not that my father has maimed

our pastor or mangled all the men
with white hair in their ears.
Oh, he's hurt them for sure,

even jokes about it at dinner.
We all love the story of the plumber
who pissed his Dickies, the way my father

tells it, holding a pitcher of water
high above his head letting a trickle,
perfectly aimed, splash into the glass.

I clap and laugh with my mouth
open wide and my head thrown back
till something in the room turns.

CHILD'S SONG

Make me the meal
for a Steel Valley rose,

string my brother's teeth
over Little Beaver Creek,

on my father's bald head
paint the price of plums,

with my sister's gold hair
light fires on the sun.

Make us rubble, O make us
dust.

Your jewelry, Mother,
has gone to rust.

DO UNTO OTHERS

How many rocks would I stack
on my brother's chest? A rock
for his beauty, a rock for his trust,

and two for lips redder
than a boy's should be.
Granite for his love

of birds; a chunk of quartz
shot through with pink.
For singing on car trips,

hiding in the dryer and flouncing
down Oak Street in my mother's dress:
limestone, shale, sandstone, flint,

limestone, shale, sandstone, flint.

Praise dead-end signs peppered with buckshot.

Praise shop windows shattered by rocks.

Praise the beige Pinto up on blocks. Praise playing chicken on
Butcher Road.

The matte black Camaro praise, and praise the '71 Chevelle:
blessed be the boy who swerves first.

Praise pig wrestling, cow tipping, cock fighting, arm wrestling, and
barn loft boxing.

Praise and praise the prom queen's ass.

Sweet corn, rhubarb, apple butter, pumpkin bread, and blackberry
jam, praise.

Praise the 606-pound squash at the county fair.

Praise bingo, scratch off lotto, and bagging the limit.

Praise the twelve-point buck strapped to Jimmy Jones' truck, friends
in orange caps gathered around, beer cans in every hand.

Praise Iron City Beer. Praise Red, White, and Blue. Praise Everclear.

Praise sniffing and huffing whatever is slapped with a warning label
or without: whip-its, whiteout, model glue, copy toner, paint
thinner, gasoline, and fat, black markers.

Praise the view at night—200 feet above the town's steeples
and oaks—from the highest rung of the water tower.

Praise the urge to jump and praise the harvest moon.

Praise flat light falling on flat land.

Praise and praise the Cuyahoga caught fire. Blessed be the man who
keeps his bobber in the water.

Praise the closed mill.

Praise the abandoned strip mine.

Praise the sign that reads DANGER: DO NOT WADE, SWIM, OR
FISH HERE! Praise, in jeans shorts and ripped concert T-shirts,
the girls who swim anyway.

Praise the jackknife, gainer, cannonball, psycho, zeeko, and
belly flop.

Praise first sex in a wood-paneled station wagon.

Praise the dirt bike and turnpike. Praise the taxidermied pike—
44 inches long and open-jawed—hung above the bar at Penn Grill.

Praise the Gin Mill, Side Door, and Hooker's Barbershop.

Praise the butch, fade, mullet, Caesar, flattop, and buzz cut.

Praise the Steel Valley. Praise the Rust Belt.

Praise the Mistake on the Lake. Praise the City on Seven Hills. Praise
the Land of Drive-Thru Liquor Stores.

Praise the home of the Fighting Quakers, Potters, Bulldogs, Warriors,
Indians, Dukes, Cardinals, and Mighty Clippers.

Praise and praise, forever and ever, the Rubber Capital of the World!

FLIGHT

I struck a match and left.
It's how I go.

A song on the radio.
A water tower in silhouette.

It's easier stealing
away than from.

A town and its horses
collapse *away*

to a single bead of light.
From: it's like tying

an anvil to a sparrow.

THE REFLECTION OF ALL VISIBLE LIGHT

The faces are white.
The flowers white.

I drive around town
expecting the familiar—deer
lashed to trucks,
kids on skates, the metal scent
of winter—

but an empty stadium
floods with light, a sky full of geese
fails.

Time is white.
The yard white.

I turn in the driveway, white
as the butcher's bar of soap.

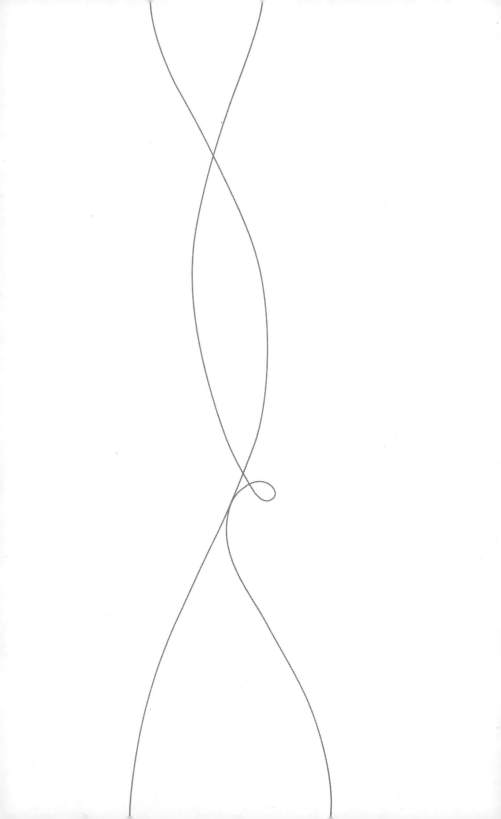

ERRATA

When I called my heart dark hammering
and your temper wild mint,
I made a mistake. I should have said

what I meant: the sucked orange

is not a symbol, nor the deer nipping
shoots outside the missile site.

It's not the year of the rat or the year of the snake

and the fat, yellow moon, despite what I whispered
at the top of the stairs, is only the moon.

I have no kinship with clouds,
no understanding of steel.

My family is becoming
a bucket of teeth

but numbers are more exact than words.

This table, this chair: I forgot
to describe this table, this chair.

Strike the word *mother* wherever you see it.

7 and 12.

Rip those pages out.

INSOMNIAC'S PSALM

Fat lot of good quitting drinking.
Fat lot of good 200 channels and six in Spanish,
or the virgin's tired face touring Kentucky:
tonight on a water tower, tomorrow
flickering on a drive-in screen.
Fat lot of good my silver-dipped tongue—
I stutter prayers and can't sit still in church.
I am ashamed, Lord, and cannot sleep.
Fat lot of good fucking slow on Sunday morning,
curtains blushed with sun.

Floods and bugs are killing us, Lord.

Fat lot of good good.

HER BODY IS A WHITE THING IN THE SUN NOW

Drum for the wind in a brown flower field

(body so soft the hoof passes through)

her hair is a nest of frost (her mouth

a hole for mice or a post)

0

Zero can hold me for days,
small sack of white,

and I hold it back,
carrying it with me, hollow

as a wing bone,
weightless as winter light.

I bring zero here—
where the wind empties

its mouth again and again,
where seabirds circle and sing,

where men squat on buckets to fish—
and it swells in me, wet days

when the boats ghost past:
a zero so large I know

I could pass my body through it.

O how the beds cricket

when you're gone
from me and this flat

full of knives.
I can't watch again

the moon's blue movies

or listen to my neighbor,
the policeman, shouting

Whose pussy is it?
Whose pussy is it?

and then a voice singing
higher and higher

Yours! Yours!

FOR EBELE

On, upon, lover & over,
these are the ways

& in, that you light
my body like

nineteen rooms
at the water's edge

LATE FOR DINNER WITH KENJI AND YOON

After stepping from the shower,
you bend your knees in a careful plié,
angling scissors toward the space
between water-dappled legs.
Sitting on the toilet, I stop
clipping my nails to watch you tease
the sopping black tuft
away from your lower belly,
scissor tips splayed in air.
Slowly, you repeat the act
I don't know what to call it—
a tiny planet of fur or a fallen nest—
lies on a bed of tissues in the bathroom trash.
I pick it up, this pagan keepsake,
roll the wool between my fingers,
smell it, joke that I will wear your sex
around my neck as an amulet
when I bike into traffic at dusk,
when I am bodyless, no more
than a blinking white light.
Brushing your teeth now
in the fogged mirror, you motion
for me to leave it, hurry up:
We're already late. We're always late.

I cup the shorn ringlets in my palm
a moment longer. Then stash them
in my jacket pocket, and call out your name,
racing down steep black steps.

APT. 2

Poured into the drain, the dregs of wine.
Wiped down, the mini blinds and toilet seat.

Boxed up, our shoes and taxes,
my insect collection, your wedding dress;

our paperclips, records, and aspirin bottles,
knives, salt, plates, books,

and dark room. This place, another, is almost gone.

But it's not the treelined street I'll miss—
it's the bedroom light switch

and the filthy nimbus ringing it.

So let the supers paint our bedroom wall
a sea of pale rose. I refuse.

HOUSE WARMING

Two mice like a pair of infant lungs,
one curled up under the butcher's cart,
the second, bloodied and jerking,
stuck by its mouth to the trap.

We are making preparations.
We are clearing a path.

In our wake, a dirty snow
of ants,
beetles,
gnats,
mosquitoes
and moths.

Come now.
Let's not forget
the nest we gassed.

The bedroom stinks of paint.
A strip of flies is twirling above the kitchen sink.

Come now.
We've lit a blinding fire.
We're reading beside it the Book of Names.

GHAZAL

You sing, bird-small, from the reeds at night.
In search, I wet my sleeves at night.

A Cooper's hawk. A red-tailed fox.
One trots, one screams—through my dreams at night.

All we have lost is brightly lost.
What flames copper green? Our grief at night.

Tongue-dumb, I was born more rock than not;
the stars like sores I can see at night.

Gin-drunk, god-sick, and opossum-quiet,
if Daniel must go, he'll leave at night.

AFTER WORDS

You won't remember the pig's head
hanging from a tree
at the end of this poem

and I, most likely, will forget

the pattern of yellow petals
blowing across
your softest sweater.

When you watch me
grip the hatchet, I become
a hatchet—

notched oak handle,
cold steel head.

When I glimpse you standing
by the woodpile and hear

you gasp, you become the gasp,

until later you become
damp smoke. Then crying.
Then whiskey.

I'm not these words, though
you think I am.

I'm taillights disappearing,

I'm what's hanging still
from a tree in brown light.

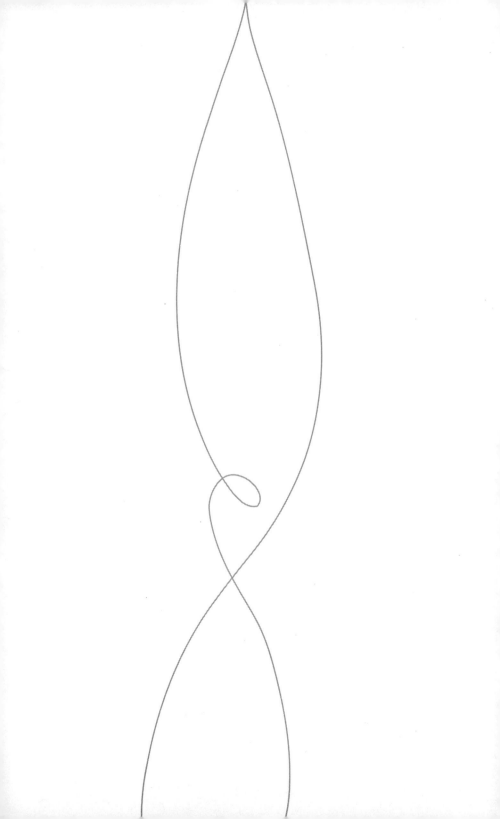

TO CATCH A FALLING KNIFE

Temple your hands
palm to palm
and hold them out.
Let slice
between your thumbs
the day's last
light.

To catch a falling knife
you have to double-doubt
the knife: its rosewood handle
doubt and doubt
its stone-ground blade,
or singing down
the knife will come
cleaving ring from pinky
finger, light from
dark and what you believe,
once and for all,
from what you don't.

To catch a falling knife

you have to believe

there is no knife.

Temple, now, your trembling hands.

FOR OSIA

I wait for you with nothing—
not figs
or a sweater,
not poem, petal,
or stone.
A loaf of bread
dark as tar.
I don't have that
either, or two
thin bones I found
by the road
while walking—

and if, against night,
Osia, you haven't come home,
I'll cup in my hands
nothing harder.

INHERITANCE

We drank hard water.
Spoke in plain language.

Said what we didn't

with a joke or a look.
One went missing—

let silence drill its hole.
A second fell ill.

We cloaked our mirrors.
Slashed a red X

on the door to our house.
Pass over us, I asked

the raven sky,
or burn in me

a second mouth.

DANIEL

When the lions did not rend him
limb from limb, his captors
raised him from the pit,
at last, and he walked
on two good legs
to his house in the rain.
He set his sandals by the door,
kissed his wife.
In a slatted chair, he sat
by the window tugging
thick tufts of beard.
The sun set. It rose.
News of his accusers came
before dusk: men,
women, and children
chewed by lions to red
rags. On the cold floor,
Daniel knelt and wept—
he was not thankless.

PRAYER FOR THE COLLECTOR OF SMALL ANIMAL SKULLS

Always Watching Light and Shadow Skinny as a Willow Switch
    are names I would choose for the boy skipping stones across
    the flooded quarry.

In high summer, his hair is milkweed silk; thrown into a well,
    his voice sinks and rises, reedy still.

Look after this child, cowlicked and burred, at least out of the corner
    of your eye. *Selah.*

Let him sit, late in the day, where he can't be seen from the house,
    Petty Thief Stripping Petals from a peony, white as winter breath:

        God is my judge. God is not. God is my judge. God is not.

Let petals snow on the lawn. Let no harm, let no harm come
to the Collector of Small Animal Skulls.

MINIATURE

A man is painting a white house
with green shutters
onto a grain of rice.
The house is a pinhead,
the shutters smaller.
Staring through a magnifying glass,
he trims his sable brush
with surgeon's scissors
and dabs China red
into the scene.
He rinses his brush
then strokes, fine as a nerve,
a plume of smoke.
It must be fall or winter.
A giant oak bare of leaves.
A station wagon parked in the street.

He mixes whites with reds
and a bit of ochre,
but it's nothing like
the rosy white
topping his knuckles.
He adds a tinge of burnt
umber—the sky outside

beginning to lighten—
and continues to paint.
In front of the house,
under the towering oak,
he adds a fleck, then
another, and one more,
until a man is standing
in front of his house.
Beside him a woman
in a blue dress.

They are small as dust
come to rest
on the blade of a razor.
Again, he snips hairs
from his triple-zero brush
and bends so close
that his breath rocks
the grain of wet rice.
He backs up, breathes,
and paints a package
or a bundle into the woman's arms.
The man pauses, paints,
then pauses, again,
painting only between
the beats of his heart.

ONE HAND KNOWS NOT WHAT
THE OTHER DOES

One hand makes nothing,
never raises wine.

Dumb twin, it sits
all day on his knee

or swings slow
circles like the hanged

at his side. Plucked wing.
Cup no good

for drinking water,
tea, or gin.

Small machine for waving
smoke from the eyes.

Who named the bones
of the hand

triquetrum, scaphoid—
as if he were ranking,

late at night,
his mistakes as a man—

Spiritus Sancti?
Hand held up to sun,

you are a map
of ruins already

open, soft.

DESCRIPTION OF A BADLY DRAWN HORSE

The horse's head looks more like the butt of an oar—
squared off and wooden the way an animal's is not.
Its mane is mangy, the mouth toothy, one white eye is wild.

The legs tangle at wrong angles, and the body stops short.
This was a horse to shoot, but I sharpened my pencil instead,
and returned to my seat. Astride the beast, with hands like clouds

and checkered shirt, rides a boy not whipping his horse,
battering its belly with shiny spurs, or scouting the dusty plains
and bluffs for a good leap-off place. He's smiling. Terribly.

WHO I WASN'T

I wasn't the Twin with an Eye Patch, the Boy with Twelve Toes,
    or the New Kid in Class Who Bit Simon's Face and Had to Be
    Psychoanalyzed;

nor was I First French Kisser, Top Salami Seller, or All-Time Long Pisser.

Ditto the Boy Purpled by a Deep Fryer.

I wasn't the Long Division Whiz with a Lisp or the Bully with a Dad
    in Jail and Lice. See, I had no claim to fame:

not perfect attendance or pubic hair; my parents didn't plummet
    from a ski lift; my brother could talk and walk.

Each day I stood alone kicking rocks off a cliff. *Would it be better*, I
    asked the puffy clouds, *to pitch myself? Or to wait for God to do it?*

FATHER SONG

A crow's been coming
to drink from my eyes,

to pluck black hairs
from my head

for a nest. He's
gentle for a crow,

his caw soft.
Before flying off

with a shock
of hair in his beak,

he'll perch on my shoulder
and preen. It's tender

almost and I,
the tendee.

AD INFINITUM

With a cotton towel white as the sun,
God is scratching grit from the pearl
handle of a pawnshop pistol.

He spit-shines the snub barrel
and stock, then stops dead—stares into space.
He gets up from his chair,

goes nowhere, sits back down.
In his ears, ten thousand church bells.
A cloud of whispers like distant surf.

He scours the tarnished trigger,
kicks open the chamber, spinning
now like a roulette wheel.

God lays the clean gun down.
Next to it, six perfect bullets
huddle on the table. Nearby another six, and so on.

AFTER LIFE

(Dead) we are lugging buckets of black
paint through the streets.
My sister (dead) stops to darken a pigeon;

my mother (dead) stoops
to smirch the steps of the church.
With bucket and brush,

this is our job. *Night is night,*
my father (dead) declares,
because it's dark,

so we run through the world,
my brother and I, (dead, dead)
painting each fleck of light

black for the rapist, black for the stars.

A PAIR OF DIRTY GLASSES

—*after Larry Levis*

Some see a wine-colored sky at the end of it,
or a bruise cast upward, bluing at the edges.

I see a pair of dirty glasses. Thumb-smudged, thick,
they lie on a table and stare sidelong at a room.

One of the arms is bent where a spring has quit
and the scene tilts to gray when I dream through the glasses—

the end won't come, it seems, into focus exactly. Inches
from the glasses, an ashtray blurs. Or is it

a dead man's wallet? The lenses, I forgot to mention,
are milky almost and I don't see anything

except for a plastic tree in the corner and under it
a shape cowering, knees drawn up, face unwashed,

but I can't make out these things for sure
so I make them up—like the great bright squares of sunlight

opening slowly now on the ceiling above me.

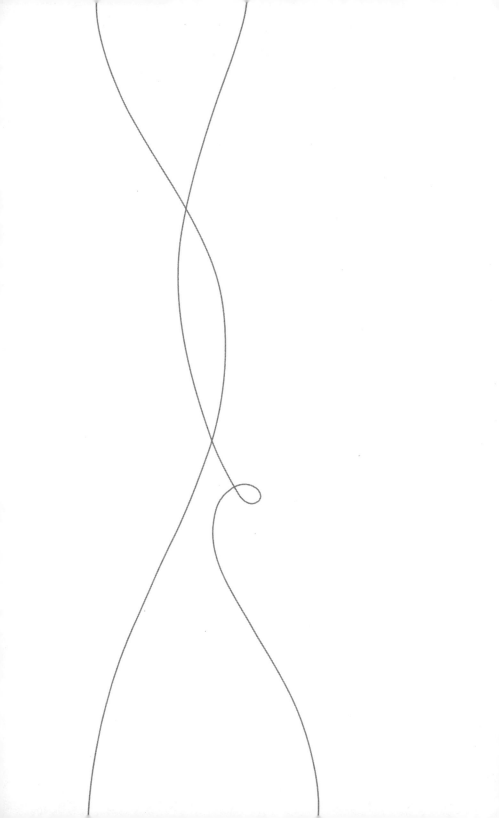

WHEN IT'S TIME

I.

I'll look up.
Take a drink of water.
Set down my cup.
When it's time.
I'll close the book I'm reading.
Leave through the sliding glass door.
Then stop.
I'll blink in hard light.
Bring my hands to my face.
Then let them fall.

II.

To the man sitting on my steps I will answer,
Wind in winter taught me to stoop.

To the bills and letters in the red-flagged box
reply, *Take my boots, my books, the jar of buttons*

and tokens, the sick orchid I nursed for weeks.
As I walk the white streets, traffic lights will blink

amber and amber. To the rusted bridge I will offer,
Here is my name weighing no more than sunlight,

my height and weight, the blue from my eyes.
When it's time, I will stand like a man at attention

and empty my pockets of keys, chap stick, pens,
a tattered notebook, and a fin of marbled jade.

When it's time, I will stare at the frozen river
and sing, *I am the son of a photograph,*

                              the son of a photograph,

until my voice sounds strange floating
like smoke into cottonwoods.

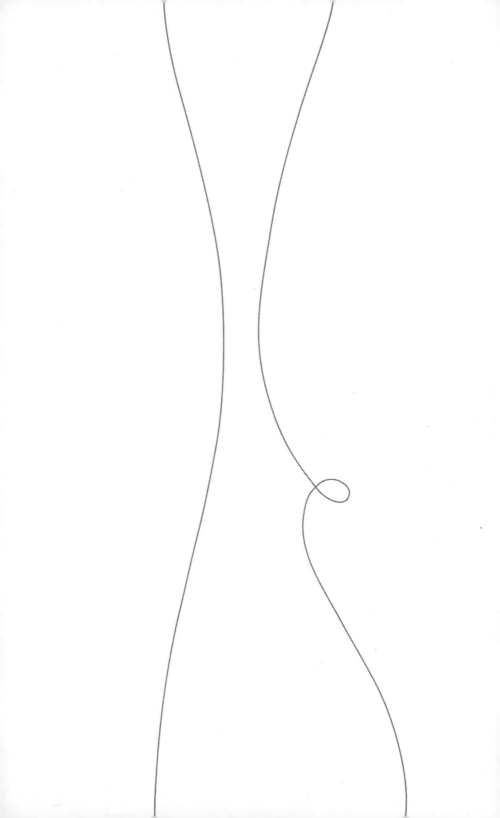

NOTES

First: The first line is Jane Mead's.

Lightweight Champion of the World: Ray "Boom Boom" Mancini–a
native of Youngstown, Ohio–defended his lightweight title
against Doo Koo Kim in a 14-round bout on November 13,
1982. Mancini won the fight. Five days later, Kim died from
brain injuries.

My Father, the Small Town Sadist: Dedicated to my father, who
practiced dentistry in the same office in Salem, Ohio for
37 years.

Visitation: "Cuyahoga" in Iroquois translates to "Crooked River,"
another name for the Ohio river that last caught fire in 1969.
Other years the polluted river caught fire: 1868, 1883, 1887,
1912, 1922, 1936, 1941, 1948, and 1952.

Her Body Is a White Thing in the Sun Now: This title borrows from
that of a poem by Larry Levis.

How to Catch a Falling Knife: Dedicated to my brother, Mark Johnson.

For Osia: This poem was composed after reading Nadezhda
Mandelstam's last letter to her husband, the poet Osip
Mandelstam, who died while serving 5 years in a Russian labor
camp for "counter-revolutionary activities."

RECENT TITLES FROM ALICE JAMES BOOKS

Phantom Noise, Brian Turner
Pageant, Joanna Fuhrman
The Bitter Withy, Donald Revell
Winter Tenor, Kevin Goodan
Slamming Open the Door, Kathleen Sheeder Bonanno
Rough Cradle, Betsy Sholl
Shelter, Carey Salerno
The Next Country, Idra Novey
Begin Anywhere, Frank Giampietro
The Usable Field, Jane Mead
King Baby, Lia Purpura
The Temple Gate Called Beautiful, David Kirby
Door to a Noisy Room, Peter Waldor
Beloved Idea, Ann Killough
The World in Place of Itself, Bill Rasmovicz
Equivocal, Julie Carr
A Thief of Strings, Donald Revell
Take What You Want, Henrietta Goodman
The Glass Age, Cole Swensen
The Case Against Happiness, Jean-Paul Pecqueur
Ruin, Cynthia Cruz
Forth A Raven, Christina Davis
The Pitch, Tom Thompson
Landscapes I & II, Lesle Lewis
Here, Bullet, Brian Turner
The Far Mosque, Kazim Ali
Gloryland, Anne Marie Macari
Polar, Dobby Gibson
Pennyweight Windows: New & Selected Poems, Donald Revell
Matadora, Sarah Gambito
In the Ghost-House Acquainted, Kevin Goodan
The Devotion Field, Claudia Keelan
Into Perfect Spheres Such Holes Are Pierced, Catherine Barnett

Alice James Books has been publishing poetry since 1973 and remains one of the few presses in the country that is run collectively. The cooperative selects manuscripts for publication primarily through regional and national annual competitions. Authors who win a Kinereth Gensler Award become active members of the cooperative board and participate in the editorial decisions of the press. The press, which historically has placed an emphasis on publishing women poets, was named for Alice James, sister of William and Henry, whose fine journal and gift for writing went unrecognized during her lifetime.

◆

TYPESET AND DESIGNED BY MARY AUSTIN SPEAKER

Printed by Thomson-Shore

on 30% postconsumer recycled paper

processed chlorine-free